MW01204203

Treasure Chest of Poems

Treasure Chest of Poems

RAYNE WAGNER

RESOURCE *Publications* · Eugene, Oregon

TREASURE CHEST OF POEMS

Resource Publications
An Imprint of Wipf and Stock Publishers
199 W. 8th Ave., Suite 3
Eugene, OR 97401

www.wipfandstock.com

PAPERBACK ISBN: 978-1-7252-7071-8
HARDCOVER ISBN: 978-1-7252-7072-5
EBOOK ISBN: 978-1-7252-7073-2

Manufactured in the U.S.A.   06/03/20

CONTENTS

HUNGRY LIONS

The lions were hungry and so we are told.
They growled and snarled, so brave and bold;
Then Daniel was thrown into the lion's den:
Counselors of the king had planned to win.

Daniel knelt right down to say his prayer
Expecting the lions to pounce on him there.
He prayed that if God was to let him die,
Then His will be done: he won't ask why.

The Lord answered his prayer. He would save;
Don't worry about the lions, but be brave.
The Lord shut their mouths all that night;
And Daniel came out of their den all right.

By Rayne Wagner
Feb. 25, 1986

CONSIDERATION

Now what have you done for anyone
   You might have seen by the way?
You say you love the one above,
   Then, why not show it today.

To show a smile across the isle
   To some one you see in church.
Don't wear a frown, or let God down
   As you now begin your search.

It's God you show by love bestowed
   To each one you chance to meet;
So don't be still, or give up till
   You have risen to your feet.

Then cross the way, do not delay;
   Get up and shake their hand.
So let them know He loves them so,
   And wants them in His band.

By Rayne Wagner
July 10, 1982

ADAM AND CHRIST

Adam looked around the garden;
None like himself could he find.
There were so many animals
Each with another of its own kind.
   "Lord have you forgotten me.
   I searched this old world over;
   Everything I find has its mate
   Down to the four leaf clover."
God knew what He was doing;
Adam was special in His sight.
Everything that God does is good;
So, what He did was all right.
   A deep sleep fell upon Adam.
   What he dreamed we do not know,
   But God performed an operation
   Because the Bible tells us so.
The results was another creation
Taken from a rib in his side.
He called this creature a woman;
Together, they would abide.
   Adam loved this woman, Eve;
   They worked in the garden together.
   Adam was happy with his wife;
   And their life would last forever.
Eve went to the forbidden tree.
Its fruit was pleasing to the eye.
She should not have been there
But was tempted the fruit to try.
   The serpent said, "It is alright
   For you will not surely die.
   Now, you can trust in me:
   For I would never tell a lie.
Whether he had told the truth,
Or if the words of God were so
Now, would she be like God
For good and evil to know?

The fruit would make one wise;
Had not a serpent just said so!
She plucked fruit from the tree,
That for sure she might know.
Eve took the fruit back to Adam,
And told him what she had done;
That she had already taken a bite;
And now that he could take one.
Adam loved his wife so much
He knew the serpent told a lie.
But how could he ever let her go
For he knew that she would die.
So Adam also bit into that fruit
To share in his wife's coming fate.
Now must all suffer this death,
For the deed was done. It's too late.
God, through His love for mankind
Had a plan ready for the Eden pair.
That all might regain that lost
And eternal life again to share.
Christ would die and man live.
For man cannot save his own life,
Nor can he saved the life of another.
No, not even that of his wife.
Christ has redeemed all of us,
That will believe on His name.
He died upon Calvary's cross
And suffered disgrace and shame.
But He rose to life immortal,
And He promised us this life too.
For all who come to Jesus Christ
He stands and waits for you.

By Rayne Wagner
1964

DAY THEN NIGHT

The clouds turn red, orange, and blue.
The night comes with its cold winds too.
The sky gets red, when the sun goes down.
And all street lights, light up the town.

All the day sounds have come and gone.
Sounds of the night have then come on.
Now it is colder, as the sun goes away.
I wish it warmer, as it was in the day.

And the moon has come out to show to me
That not all the light has gone, you see.
But now the night has come and gone,
For the daylight too is coming back on.

By Rayne Wagner
June 18, 1964

HE PAID THE PRICE

A wonderful Saviour is Jesus.
   Oh what a friend is He.
He died upon a cruel cross,
   And paid the price for me.
None other but Jesus Christ
   Could wash my sins away.
He paid the price for all
   That are living here today.
There is no better tomorrow
   We could make on our own.
He could make the sacrifice,
   And for all our sins atone.
Do you wish for a better life
   Than you are living today?
Surrender all your sins to God;
   Just kneel down and pray.
He can be your loving Saviour.
   A true friend to you too.
Let Him come into your heart.
   He is waiting now for you.
Can't you hear Him calling,
   "Come, dear one to me?
But do not fear of falling."
   He holds our hand, you see.

By Rayne Wagner

JESUS LOVES

Yes, Jesus has died for you and me
On an old rugged cross of Calvary.
It's a symbol of His undying love
That Jesus now gives us from above.

I know that He loves me, you see
Because of what He's done for me.
The Lord has His outstretched hand
For each one who takes their stand.

He wants us to have a life of love,
As He is now giving us from above.
Will you join with me now and pray
That we will see that city someday?

By Rayne Wagner

POOR LOST DOG

A little lost dog I have found.
She doesn't know her way around.
She seems so lost and all alone.
No place she can call her own.

I thought she was cute, you see.
Walking up to a stranger like me.
She slept the whole night through
Knowing that here was a friend too.

She was thirsty which I could tell.
And she was not feeling very well.
So I could not leave her all alone,
Knowing that she had lost her home.

And if she would not run away,
I'll find a home for her to stay.
Now she is laying on the seat
Waiting for her master to meet.

By Rayne Wagner

THE WORD OF GOD

God made the earth and it went around.
When He made it, there was not a sound.
The earth was dark, and you couldn't see.
God wanted light, He said, "Let it be."

He called one half day; the other night,
This made His work come out just right.
God wanted a heaven about this earth,
Which was a part of this world's birth.

One would think this was a lot to do,
But He spoke a word, and made land too.
There were no plants anywhere it seems;
So He made those things by His own means.

He made the sun and moon for many reasons:
For our signs, the days, and the seasons.
Now, things were a little bit too still;
So He made some animals just by His will.

He made animal's for land, air, and sea.
And then He made a man their ruler to be.
He finished His work after the sixth day.
On the seventh He says, worship His way.

Now, the Devil did tempt Eve into sin;
And now, that is how the world has been.
Christ died so our sins could be forgiven;
He has prepared for us a home in heaven.

And so I hope you are now willing to be
That kind of Christian God wants to see.
You can see all that He has done for you;
So, now, try to live your life anew.

By Rayne Wagner

TO BUILD A NEST

To watch a bird build a nest
Is an exciting thing to see.
It works hard to make it best
For the mother bird to be.

In this nest are some eggs.
Count them: one, two, three.
Out pokes their little heads;
And, soon, they will be free.

They will test their wings,
And fly in the sky so blue.
I can hear them as they sing.
Their song is clear and true.

And, as time goes swiftly by,
They will want to build a nest,
To have some little ones fly;
And make their nest the best.

By Rayne Wagner

WORLD AT AN END

All glory to God our Father
Through whom all power flows.
He sent His dear Son Jesus
With whom His love bestows.

Jesus lived upon this earth
With a life free from sin.
He died for each one of us
That we might live with Him.

At the end of this old world
When righteous ones are raised,
All the wicked are then slain,
God will receive His praise.

Then, will the universe know
That God's law is justified;
And Satan has lied about Him.
God's name will be glorified.

By Rayne Wagner

BIRTH OF CHRIST

A star stood brightly shinning in the sky.
   It looked so close, yet up so high.
It began to drift along through the night.
   Wise men followed, so not to lose sight.
It wandered to a little town, far away;
   There above a stable it seemed to stay.
The star seemed to dance about with glee
   Such wonder in the stable it now did see.
There was a little baby lying in a manger.
   Every one there seemed like a stranger.
The shepherds came to see Him lying there
   Without much worry, or any care.
Now, soon this baby would grow to be a man.
   He would carry the burdens of the land.
And His love would flow freely to every one
   This baby was Christ, God's beloved son.
Love was the one talent that God did show;
   It's one which every one can bestow.
Like a star let your heart dance with glee.
   With the love Christ showed to you and me.

By Rayne Wagner

THE KING IS COMING

Lift up your head unto the sky
Tis the King who comes from on high.
   Now raise your voices to the Lord
He comes to give us our reward.

   The trumpet blows out loud and clear
The dead are raised: all them who hear
   The words, "come forth to life anew
All ye who listen, My faithful few.

   Ye are free. I have paid the cost.
I have redeemed that which was lost.
   The earth is mine, and all therein.
And, sin shall not rise up again.

   All who are alive on that day,
Will bow the knee, and there to pray.
   All will acknowledge that God is true
When He comes down from skies of blue.

   The night is long, but day is nearing
When we shall see our Saviour appearing.
   At first we'll see a cloud so small;
Then it will grow to be seen by all.

   The saints will shout, "Victory is nigh,
Death where is thy sting, they will cry."
   Then graves are opened, and many arise
To be with the Lord, up in the skies.

   The earth is crowned with His glory.
And Saints tell the redemptive story.
   We will grow up as calves in a stall.
Christ our King will reign over all.

Are you waiting, and bowed in prayer,
Or will the Lord catch you unaware?
Are you just doing your everyday thing;
Thinking little about the coming King?

Time is short, and the Lord in near.
Do not wait until Christ does appear.
Now is salvation, Jesus calls for you
So, really, what do you plan to do?

By Rayne Wagner

PUT YOUR TRUST IN JESUS

Don't worry about tomorrow
Don't make the heart feel sad
Just put your trust in Jesus
He'll make the heart feel glad.

You want someone to love you
Just like a friend should do
Then put your trust in Jesus
He'll be that friend to you.

There is no one like Jesus
In this wide world around
And He loves you very much
Greater love cannot be found.

He is always there to listen
So to hear your every plea
Now put your trust in Jesus
To calm your troubled sea.

Don't worry about tomorrow
And wipe those tears away
So put your trust in Jesus
And live for Him today.

By Rayne Wagner

GOD'S GARDEN

God made a garden, bright and green.
The prettiest garden ever seen.
Everything planted by His own hand
From a blade of grass to a grain of sand.

He entrusted it all for us to name.
Each kind of flower, each kind of grain.
He left it for man to take special care
That beautiful garden God did share.

Now as we look at this world today
Where is that garden people seem to say?
Where is this home that Adam once had?
Where is that garden to make us glad?

God could not stand to see such waste
Just because of man's change of taste;
So He moved it from this world today,
Man would have destroyed it anyway.

By Rayne Wagner

PORTRAIT OF JESUS

A portrait of Jesus hangs on my wall
Some of them large, some are small.
Oh, to see the beauty of each face
Hanging there with such loving grace.

A picture of His outstretched hands
Stretching over earth's many lands
Hoping some will answer His call
Before their sins cause their fall.

We now see Him praying by the way
Just before that crucifixion day
Think of the troubles He went through
Because of His love, for me, and you.

When ever we see Him coming again
I am sure we will all say, "Amen."
He'll take us to that city so grand
Beyond this sinful, earthly land.

When we see His face shining bright
Then we'll know everything's all right.
Of all the troubles we've gone through
There is not one He hasn't faced too.

By Rayne Wagner

EVERLASTING BEAUTY

I painted a picture of an evergreen tree
Its everlasting beauty people might see
I painted it out in nature's land
Which was all created by God's own hand.
I saw beautiful flowers everywhere
With many colors for us all to share.

Then I saw a lake so peaceful and blue
And God gave it His special color too.
Then I saw white clouds hanging above
Another thing just to show Gods love.
I see far off those mountains so tall
Taller and higher than the highest wall.

God placed these scenes here to see
Because He wants to show His love to me.
I have painted this picture here for you
So that you may see all its beauty too.
I can't paint the picture like God has done
But I tried my best just to paint this one.

By Rayne Wagner

HOMELAND

I know of a homeland far from this earth
A land of beauty beyond compare or worth
It's a land everyone would like to see
Where only the righteous will ever be.
   All the walls are made of precious gems
   With the righteous singing glorious hymns
   And within the walls is the tree of life
   Where the righteous have no worry or strife.
A river of life flowing out from God
Where so many people are seen to trod.
Where the beauty of nature is all around
Just only in heaven can there be found.
   There'll be an absence of sickness and care
   For Jesus the fairest of all will be there
   Abraham, Noah, Daniel and all the rest
   Will be there among those that are blessed.
But we must shake off our life of sin
Before to heaven we can enter in
We will put on the cloak of immortality
Our bodies will be filled with vitality.
   For we will never grow old and weary,
   Or have our days be dark and dreary
   Forever to have such blissfulness
   In heaven our home eternal happiness.

By Rayne Wagner

END OF TIME

I looked down on this world I have created
A long time its destruction I have debated
Should I let them live a little longer
Or would sin become a little stronger?

I have tried throughout the countless ages
To end this war of sin the devil wages
For I know that he has claimed quite a few
Who have yielded to his point of view.

In the final hour time will cease to be
Too late for them to ever turn again to me
For they chosen the path they wanted to go
I will say to them, "You, I do not know."

I will rejoice for the one sinner saved
Even though there are many who misbehaved.
In the end they had made their own choice.
Listening to the devil instead of God's voice.

I challenge you friend in earth's final hour
To obey My words or be held by Satan's power
Time is drawing fast and quickly to an end
Which voice will you listen to now my friend?

By Rayne Wagner

LEAVES OF GOLD

The leaves are falling on the ground
Their colors are red, gold, and brown
I love to watch them as they fall
Even though I can't see them all.

I know the days will soon turn cold
When I do see those leaves of gold.
The small trees shake and tremble so
As the fall winds then start to blow.

Now that fall has come and gone
That time of year which I am fond
Still I won't fret or show any fear
As I know fall will come next year.

The rains will come and turn to snow
Then fall will be over, this I know
I will miss my pretty leaves of gold
Whenever the weather does turn cold.

By Rayne Wagner

I AM THE VINE

I am the vine and ye are the branches
For he that abideth in me shall live
If anyone thirst, let him come to Me.
Just ask of me, and I'll freely give.

I am the vine and ye are the branches
In Me you'll find strength and stay
And even though I have grafted you in
You should trust in Me to lead the way.

I am the vine and ye are the branches
The same shall bring forth much fruit
Without Me, ye cannot do anything
The nourishment comes from the root.

I am the vine and ye are the branches
And he that does not abide in Me
Shall be cast forth and wither and die
Without Me there's no life you see.

By Rayne Wagner

GOD SAYS

God says, "Let there be dark
   And let there be light."
Then He called one "day",
   And the other one, "night".

Then God put a rainbow
   To appear in the sky
Just to show us the beauty
   In that great by and by.

God made the animals
   Each one two by two
Every creature on the earth
   For the benefit of you.

God looks down upon us
   As faithful as can be
In hopes we'd be grateful
   And live so happily.

While we are all quarreling
   About out thoughtless whims
Some are asking for His help
   Pleading help from Him.

Yes, our God forgives us
   He tries to make it right
Do we ask in earnest prayer
   For God to stop the fight?

The world and all there is
   Was made by God's own Son.
Look at the mess there is today
   Just see what we've done.

By Rayne Wagner

MESSAGE FROM JESUS

Oh My people, how long must I plead
For you to turn to me when in need?
You look to self until all else fails;
Then call on Me with moans and wails.

You talk about and against each other.
Not willing to save your own brother.
If you want for this old world to end,
Take Christ to each one who has sinned.

Make it your goal every minute each day.
Lead one to Christ, it's the only way.
Turn to Jesus, put Him first in mind;
His goodness and mercy you will find.

By Rayne Wagner

OH LORD LET ME IN

Oh lord, let me in, let me in.
For I am just a victim of sin
I've been this way all my life
Nothing here but worry and strife.

Don't send me to an early grave.
Oh Lord I'll promise to behave
Don't tell me Lord it's too late
Please don't shut the golden gate.

Oh Lord, let me in, let me in
You know what my life has been
Lord I want to be by your side
No more sin, and no more pride.

I will walk in the right way
If Lord you'll let me in today
I promise that I will be good.
Just as any good man should.

Please, Lord, don't let me down
I want to be in that Holy town
You promised that you'd forgive
So please Lord there let me live.

Oh lord, let me in, let me in
Don't leave me in a world of sin
I want to hear the angels sing
And hear those church bells ring.

So, now, tell me Lord I do pray
If you'll open up the gates today.
I won't let that old devil win.
Oh lord, let me in, let me in.

By Rayne Wagner

BOUND FOR THE KINGDOM

I'm bound for the kingdom
This is one race I can win.
A crown is laid up for me
I've got victory over sin.

Jesus will be my king there
He will reign over my life
I'll bear the cross He bore
In times of worry and strife.

I've made my choice with Jesus
And I chose the better land.
It's not like this old world
It's one so glorious and grand.

Although the road is not easy
I'm still pressing for that goal
Nothing will ever detain me
I don't plan to lose my soul.

Jesus is to be my guide now
That I may not lose the way
He'll always stand beside me
Throughout each and every day.

By Rayne Wagner

WHO IS JESUS?

What does Jesus mean to you?
Was He just a man, kind and true?
He healed the sick wherever He went
Was He your Saviour, from God sent?

If He was a man kind and true
And died a death as others do
Then all the world worships in vain
For they too shall not live again.

If He is God's only begotten Son
Then the battle against death is won
For if your sins He does forgive
You'll have a chance again to live.

If you take Jesus as your Saviour
Then let it show in your behavior
For only through your love for God
The heavenly streets you will trod.

By Rayne Wagner

TO BE A CHRISTIAN

To be a Christian
One must know how to love
   To be a Christian
   We must love the God above.
To be a Christian
We must then obey His laws.
   To be a Christian
   There must not be any flaws.
To be a Christian
Believe Christ is your Saviour.
   To be a Christian
   We must have the right behavior.
To be a Christian
We now must be born again.
   To be a Christian
   We must not ever want to sin.
To be a Christian
Want to live in God's homeland.
   To be a Christian
   We must join the Christian band.

By Rayne Wagner

A WAY TO HEAVEN

Show me a way to heaven
Up in the starry blue.
Show me a way to heaven
Where all things are new.

I want to be near Jesus
Tell me how to get there.
Seeing the things you've done
It is then I know you care.

Show me the way to heaven
I know this you can do
Show me the way to heaven
For I know you love me too.

By Rayne Wagner

STARS IN CHRIST'S OWN CROWN

I stand gazing up in the sky.
   I see some stars way up high.
Like little diamonds in the night.
   Shining down pretty and bright.

God put them here for you and me:
   Right there for our joy, you see.
They were put there for us a light
   To shine through the dark of night.

They are stars in Christ's own crown.
   They are known the world around.
God put them there for us to see.
   For every one, for you, and me.

By Rayne Wagner

BURNING LIGHT

You have set a light a burning
   To guide me on my way.
For my heart is ever yearning
   To be with you some day.

I see the work of your hands
   That everyone can see,
Just as countless as the sands,
   Along an endless sea.

You have set a burning light,
   So I won't lose my way,
That I may never lose sight
   Of that glorious day.

By Rayne Wagner

THE LITTLE BOX

I found a little box there
Buried deep in the ground;
And when I opened it up
To my surprise I found:
   It was full of greed, envy,
   And it was full of hate.
   I tried to close the lid,
   But it was way too late.
They crawled all over me,
And got down deep inside,
To find the other sins
That I had tried to hide.
   Then, it made me very mad,
   To find the sins I buried,
   Were the same sins I found.
   The ones that I had carried.
So, it is hopeless to bury
Your sins in the ground
Because there'll be a day
They will again be found.
   It seems you can't get rid
   Of your sins just anywhere,
   But only through the Saviour,
   By asking Him in prayer.

   By Rayne Wagner

THE DAY IS DAWNING

The day is dawning
So bright and gay.
You wake up yawning
Ready to start the day.

The sun shines through
To brighten up my day.
It brings warmth too
To help me on my way.

By Rayne Wagner

A FLASHING LIGHT

I saw a light a flashing.
Off and on it would go.
It seemed to say, "Caution
And that is what I show."

As it flashes out its signal,
For all who may come to see,
It tells about some danger
And careless you will not be.

By Rayne Wagner

I ACKNOWLEDGE GOD

I stood very firm on my belief
That Christ is our only relief.
But God deserves some credit too.
For troubles we put Him through.

Now why should we push God aside,
For when we entered sin He cried?
Lord God we should acknowledge thee,
As a loving God, forever more to be.

By Rayne Wagner

OLD AND WEARY

I saw the old and weary laid to rest today,
For death has taken all life's cares away.
There'll be no sickness, worry, or strife
That they had to face in their daily life.

Although they have left this world behind,
They may someday a better world to find.
Do not sorrow and grieve your life away
For you might be with them again someday.

It is hard to see a loved one have to go.
You wish you could say, "it was not so."
But they are gone; they have passed away;
And left you to carry on for them today.

By Rayne Wagner

COME OUT WITH ME

Come out with me, is the call
Be a preacher, no not at all,
Just show what Christ can give,
It is eternal life to live.

Knock, and say, "how do you do.
I'm asking questions, just a few."
They may say, "Yes", or "no",
But always a smile you show.

Then, the choice is up to them.
If they will want Christ within,
So, now, come out with me,
For it is not hard, you see.

By Rayne Wagner

A SOUND IN THE NIGHT

There came a sound in a cold wintery night
That filled my soul with a fearful fright.
The dogs barked and made and awful sound.
It shook me up, and I looked all around.

I went to the window just in time to see
A most ferocious face looking back at me;
And so I ran and jumped right into my bed.
Quickly I covered all up, even to my head.

I then peeked out to see if it was there.
It disappeared; I didn't see it anywhere.
I am ashamed now, that I would run away
Because he was afraid of me on that day.

By Rayne Wagner

KING OF GLORY

Hail, hail the king of glory
   The redeemer of mankind.
We tell the redemption story
   That all, may Jesus find.

Hail, hail to our king divine
   Who rose up from the grave?
He died for your sins and mine,
   That the world, He might save.

Hail, hail the prince of peace
   For His goodness and His grace.
It is in Him we find release
   From all the troubles we face.

By Rayne Wagner

SHOW ME THE WAY

So you want to get to God's heaven.
   You better start to live right.
You want to know the way to heaven.
   It is going to be a tough fight.

If you want to get to God's heaven,
   Just don't turn your back on Me,
Or don't start listening to Satan,
   In heaven he's not going to be.

Now that you know the way to heaven;
   And you know what you have to do;
Then start by doing what is right;
   And you just might get there too.

By Rayne Wagner

WONDERFUL SAVIOUR

There was a man of Galilee.
   Oh what a man was he.
He walked upon the waters,
   And made a blind man see.

Oh what a beautiful Saviour.
   Oh what a friend was He.
He was hung on a cruel cross,
   And there He died for me.

There was a man on a hill
   And 5,000 people were fed
With just five little fishes
   And two loaves of bread.

By Rayne Wagner

GOD MADE THE EARTH

God made the earth as round as a ball.
He made the earth from nothing at all.
Jesus made the earth for Adam and Eve.
And, many blessing they did receive.

But Satan gave them something to do,
And this made Adam and Eve very blue.
They had to leave their garden home.
The world, forever, thy now will roam.

But Christ came and He died on Calvary
That they might again their home to see.
And, of course, we are all waiting too
To see that home that they once knew.

By Rayne Wagner

A BABY

You can see your baby growing up.
It's able to hold its own cup.
It still wipes food in its hair;
This is enough to make you swear.

But this is mommy's little doll
Who likes to climb up every wall?
It starts out so nice and clean,
But now it's a sight to be seen.

It's time for baby to go to sleep.
And you are so happy you can weep.
So mommy's darling is now in bed.
But that is what I thought I said.

Now this day is almost through,
And, so, I guess that you are too.
Everything is silent, not a peep.
At last the baby has gone to sleep.

By Rayne Wagner

LOOK, HEAR, AND SEE

To look upon a mountain
Up there so very high.
To see its mighty stature
Rising high in the sky.

To look upon a mighty wave,
As it rolls across the sea.
To hear it's pounding surf
There, forevermore, to be.

To look upon a wheat field
So very thick and tall.
You could almost imagine
To walk upon it and not fall.

To hear the mighty winds
Whip through the trees.
Or it can always be such
A little gentle breeze.

By Rayne Wagner

HI LONESOME

Now, here is a word to cheer you;
To keep you from being so blue.
Clouds need not be full of despair,
For the God who made them is there.

The days may be dark on the outside,
But inside there's a shining light.
The mind is like and endless ocean.
It stretches way far out of sight.

So, man cannot forget the things
That he can touch, or taste, or see.
It's only those things not around
That fades away from his memory.

For so as long as you are around
There are those who still love you.
So please, do not be so unhappy.
Don't let those skies make you blue.

By Rayne Wagner

LOVE OF GOD

To have the love of God is so grand.
   It's not hard, just take His hand.
He asks you to love one another too.
   It is not such a hard thing to do.

God loved you; Christ's life He gave
   That your life He then might save.
Please do not hate your fellow man:
   This was not in God's great plan.

Today, show your love to one another.
   It might be an angel or brother.
We must show love within our heart;
   And never to let it drift apart.

Tell of God's love that you do know;
   Then you begin your love to show.
God always hears every word we say:
   Let them be of love, this I pray.

By Rayne Wagner

PEACE OF HEART, PEACE OF MIND

Oh peace of heart, peace of mind
My love, how can you be so unkind?
We quarreled and, then, you said,
That now, we could never really wed.

My love you are so very dear to me
No other can mean so much, you see
I know that I have been so untrue,
But my love can be only for you.

Please forgive me for what I've done:
For without you, there is no more fun.
I have wandered the whole world through,
But nothing can take the place of you.

Let me have peace of heart and mind
Knowing again, your love I will find.
Let us, then, have an everlasting love
Even lasting to our heavenly home above.

By Rayne Wagner

THE QUESTION

I saw a dirty faced little boy today
Standing on the corner of the street
He was holding out his little hand
As our eyes they did chance to meet.

The little boy was dressed in rags
With pleading eyes he looked at me.
I knew he had no one who would care
By the way he was dressed, you see.

He said, "Why must I live this way;
And why has God allowed this to be?
Must it always have to be this way:
To always have to live in misery?

This life, it doesn't have to be
If people would just stop and see
What kind of life around them lives
There might not be so much misery.

By Rayne Wagner

LIGHT ON THE HILL

I saw a light on a far hill
Where everything was still
Then thunder begin to sound;
Black clouds gathered around.

The light was Jesus Christ
Who His life has sacrificed
He died there on Calvary
Just to set everyone free.

His light still shines through;
So don't feel so sad and blue.
Jesus is now in heaven above
Sending down His endless love.

He'll come back again some day
To take all our cares away;
So tell others of His light
That they might see this sight.

By Rayne Wagner

THE SCENE

I looked out across the lake.
It was so beautiful and blue
And there I saw the moonlight
Adding its silvery streak too.

How I love to hear cool waters
Washing up to the sandy shore
You can almost hear it saying
I want more room, more, more.

Over there in the far distance
You see the pine trees so green
It makes such a pretty picture
Though it, I have never seen.

You ask me how I can tell you
About such a beautiful scene
Because I had just told you
The picture I had never seen.

But I can see it real clear now
For it is here within my mind
Someday I hope to see this place,
But not now, because I am blind.

By Rayne Wagner

GOD'S CREATION

I made the darkness and the night;
I made the sun, and then the light.
And I found that it was all good,
As all thing that I made should
   But something was not there.
I made a world and hung it in space,
But on it I could not see any face;
So I made the mountains and the sea;
And I made the air as it should be,
   But something was not there.
So I made the flowers and the trees;
I then made the birds and the bees.
I made the fish in the ocean blue.
I made animals to roam the land too,
   But something was not there.
So I made a man and gave him a wife
To help him through his long life
They had a choice between good and bad.
They chose the wrong one, which is sad.
   But something was not there.
I gave my Son to die for their sin
That they might a new life to begin.
Now, if they will live a good life too,
Then My acquaintance I will again renew.
   The hope of Salvation is there.

By Rayne Wagner

GLORY TO THE LORD

When those church bells start to ringing
And, then, we all begin to singing,
Glory to the Lord, Glory to the Lord.
When the preacher starts to preaching;
Then your soul begins an upward reaching
For the glory of the Lord, Glory of the Lord.

When you are kneeling down to praying;
And you can hear those angels saying,
Glory to the Lord, Glory to the Lord;
And when you've got your mind on God,
It seems a familiar road you've trod;
Then you'll know the glory of the Lord.

And, when the angels see you coming,
They will know the tune you're humming,
Glory to the Lord, Glory to the Lord.
And when you get to heaven up there,
Then you'll have no more worry or care
For you'll see the glory of the Lord.

By Rayne Wagner

WHAT TO SAY

Dear Jesus, I want to say to Thee
What all is in my heart, you see,
But I don't find it so easy to be
Now just what is the matter with me?

Why is it that I am acting this way?
What is the matter with me today?
Why can't I say what I do feel?
This, to me, just cannot be real.

Now, how can this possibly be
For this cannot really be me.
I just want to stop and to pray,
But, then, what can I possibly say?

How to express my love for Thee.
To say it, is my problem you see.
Oh for the words that I can say
To express my feelings for you today.

My love for Jesus, is like a song
That I could sing all the day long.
My heart is like and opened book;
So come on in Lord and take a look.

You can see just what I want to say
I guess there is just no other way
To show my love for You, from me
I guess that's the way it'll always be.

For, how to say it, I do not know.
How to express it, this I can show;
And, so I'll show my love to You
Just by being a good Christian too.

By Rayne Wagner

JESUS IS COMING

Jesus is coming in all His glory
Now this is the redemptive story
All His angels then will come too
For to collect all the faithful few.

All the wicked stare in unbelief
And for them there is no relief.
A Saviour they have rejected too;
Jesus says to them I know not you.

The saints have waited for so long
Suffering from a vengeful throng.
They look up at Jesus and they see,
And shout to Jesus, you saved me.

All the dead in Christ are risen too:
Now are to be given life again anew.
All the wicked are left here to die;
And all righteous ascend to the sky.

By Rayne Wagner

ARE YOU READY?

Now are you ready
For the Lord to come?
Are all your sins forgiven?
None are left, no not one.

At the last trump
We shall be changed.
But what is left;
What has remained?

Are we doing God's will?
Are we ready to go?
Are our characters fixed?
What will our lives show?

Did we study the Bible
To know what's right,
Or listen to others,
And be lost in His sight?

By Rayne Wagner

COMING IN GLORY

Jesus is coming in all His glory;
And there is a redemptive story.
He comes with angels streaming
Down from the sky a light beaming.

The heaven are to all pass away.
The evils of the world kept at bay.
The righteous will call His name.
The wicked will others to blame.

Where will you be on that day
When Jesus takes the righteous away?
What is left of the all broken down:
The wicked dead and only Satan around?

By Rayne Wagner